a little guide to
First Communion

written by Tracy Young and illustrated by John Schafer

A Little Guide to First Communion
Copyright © 2011 by Tracy Young

All rights reserved. No part of this book may be used or reproduced in any manner whatsoever without prior written permission from the publisher except in the case of brief quotations embodied in critical articles and reviews. Published by S&V Press, a division of Sweerts & Vaas.
www.sweertsandvaas.com

ISBN:0-9822-6583-2
ISBN-13: 978-0982265833
Library of Congress Control Number: 2011925068

First Edition

This book is dedicated to
my mother

This year is especially important. Seraphina is making her First Communion.

Here we are, Seraphina.
I'll pick you and your sister up after religious education.

What did you discuss?

That thing you have to do before First Communion.

Do you mean Reconciliation?

Mom, remember when I made Sophie cry? I don't want to tell Father Jerome EVERYTHING.

Don't worry, he isn't going to judge you, but you need to remember that Communion has both inner and outer aspects.

"Mother, look at this one."

"That's beautiful. I love the pearls around the waist."

Seraphina, can you tell me the importance of First Communion?

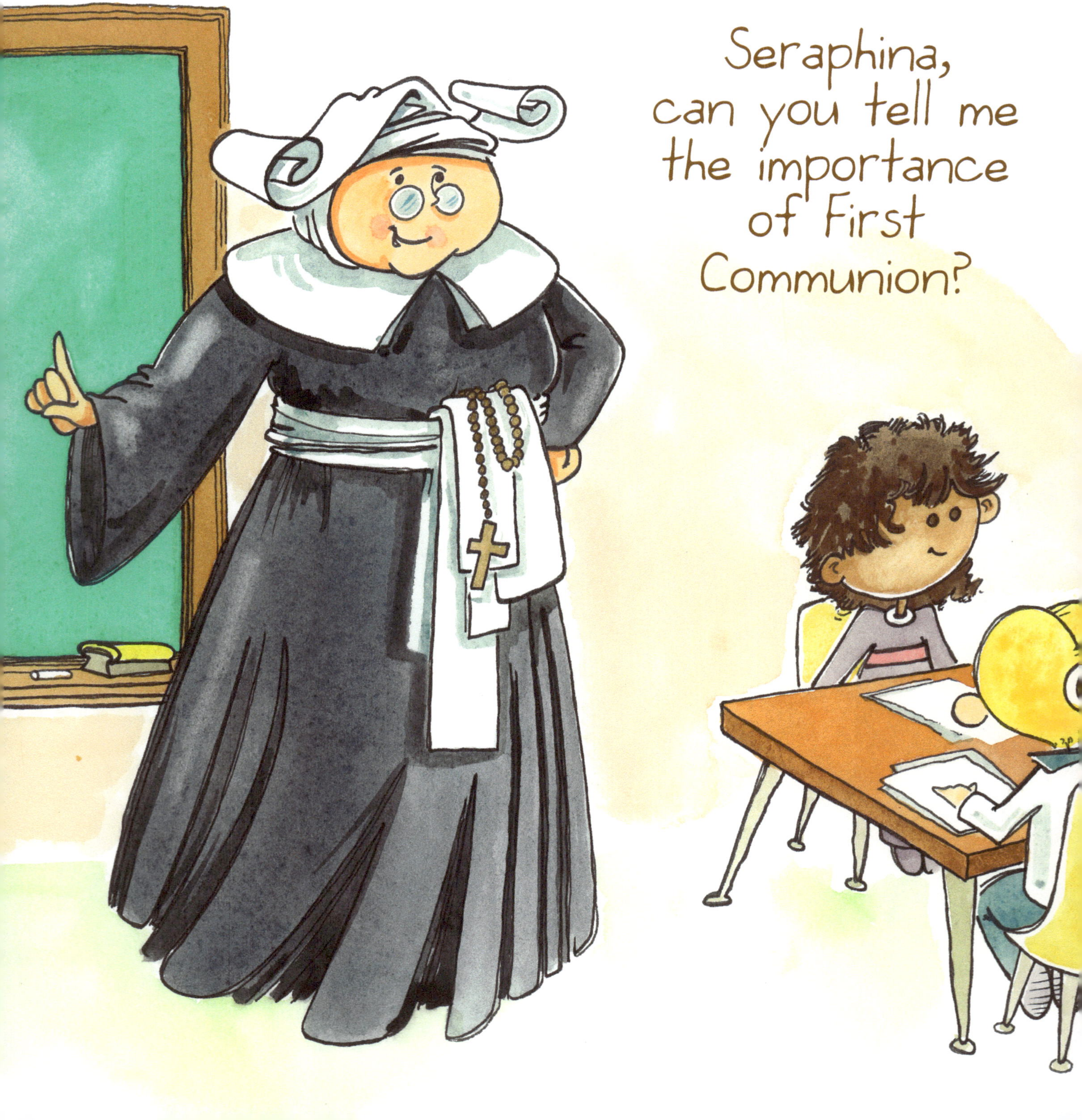

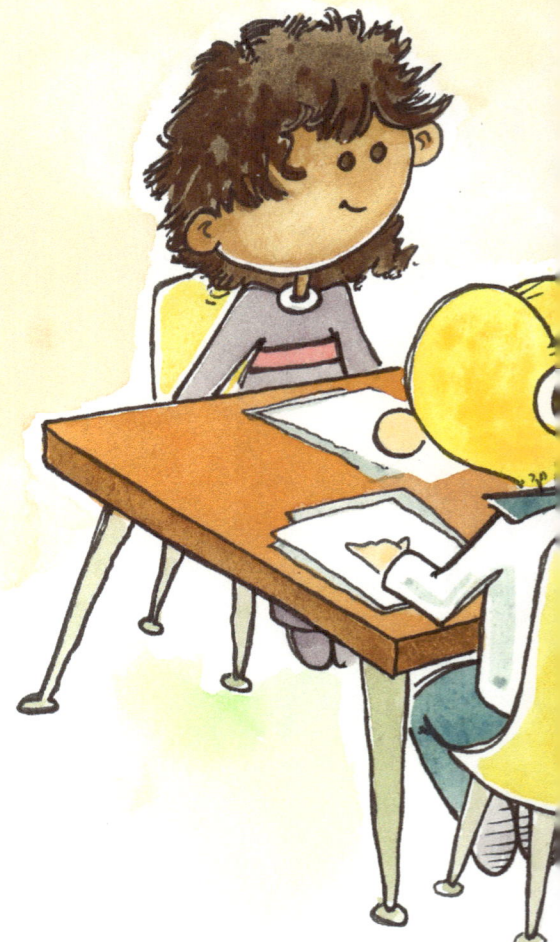

I get to wear a beautiful dress,
have a big party
and get LOTS of presents.

Perhaps you could focus on the meaning of Communion rather than the fashion element.

Since Seraphina wrote such a moving essay, she'll be doing one of the readings.
Remember to practice.

Time for dinner.

croak.

A reading from...

It is believed that
Communion originated from the Last Supper,
in which Christ celebrated the Jewish feast of
Passover with his disciples.

During the meal, he broke bread, shared wine with
the apostles, and predicted that it would be his
last meal. Today, Christ's sacrifice is remembered
when a person receives the Eucharist.

Christians all over the world share a belief in Communion, although interpretations and traditions surrounding the practice may differ.

In the Episcopalian Church, anyone who is baptized may partake in Communion. In the Eastern Orthodox as well as in the Eastern Catholic Church, Baptism, Communion and Confirmation are administered at the same time to an infant.

In the Roman Catholic church these sacraments are celebrated separately, with Baptism administered first, traditionally to an infant. Communion usually takes place when a child is between the ages of 7 and 10, while Confirmation occurs when a child is close to 15 years of age.

When making Communion, a girl traditionally wears a white dress. Styles of dresses have evolved along with fashion, of course, and today there are three types of Communion dresses: traditional, classic and modern.

Traditional Communion dresses tend to be formal, lavish and gown-length. This style is sometimes called "old world" because these dresses resemble the elaborate attire worn for Communion in some European countries. Classic Communion dresses are less elaborate than traditional dresses, but they are still quite formal. These dresses tend to have delicate bead and pearl work, and are usually tea- or ballerina-length. Lastly, modern Communion dresses have simple silhouettes, less embellishment, and end around the knee. When selecting the right outfit for her special day, it's a good idea to take your daughter's personality into consideration.

While Catholic women are no longer required to wear head coverings at Mass (unless visiting the Vatican!), some parishes continue to preserve the tradition for Holy Communion.

A traditional option is to wear a Communion veil, which is available in several lengths. Short Communion veils fall just to the shoulders, and are perfect for girls who would rather not wear anything but are required to wear a veil. Medium-length Communion veils fall below the shoulders and look charming with classic and modern styles of dresses. Finally, long veils drape down the back, with some mantilla-style veils extending all the way to the floor.

Veils are usually attached to headbands and wreaths or simply secured in the hair with bobby pins and combs. The religious instructor at each parish will detail the dress code and the head covering requirements.

A floral wreath
is another head covering option which may be worn instead of a veil. Flowers are abundant in the spring and offer a very sweet head covering for the Communion ceremony.

The floral wreath should be ordered through a florist at least a week before the event. It can be helpful to visit the florist with the child so the florist can take the child's head measurement. If that is not possible, use a tape measure to determine the head circumference right above the ears. Measure to the nearest 1/4 inch. It can be helpful to bring a picture of the dress to inspire the florist designing the wreath.

If a floral wreath feels too elaborate, a few small flowers in the hair may be all that's needed. Discuss the delivery date and time with the florist, along with proper care instructions for the flowers.

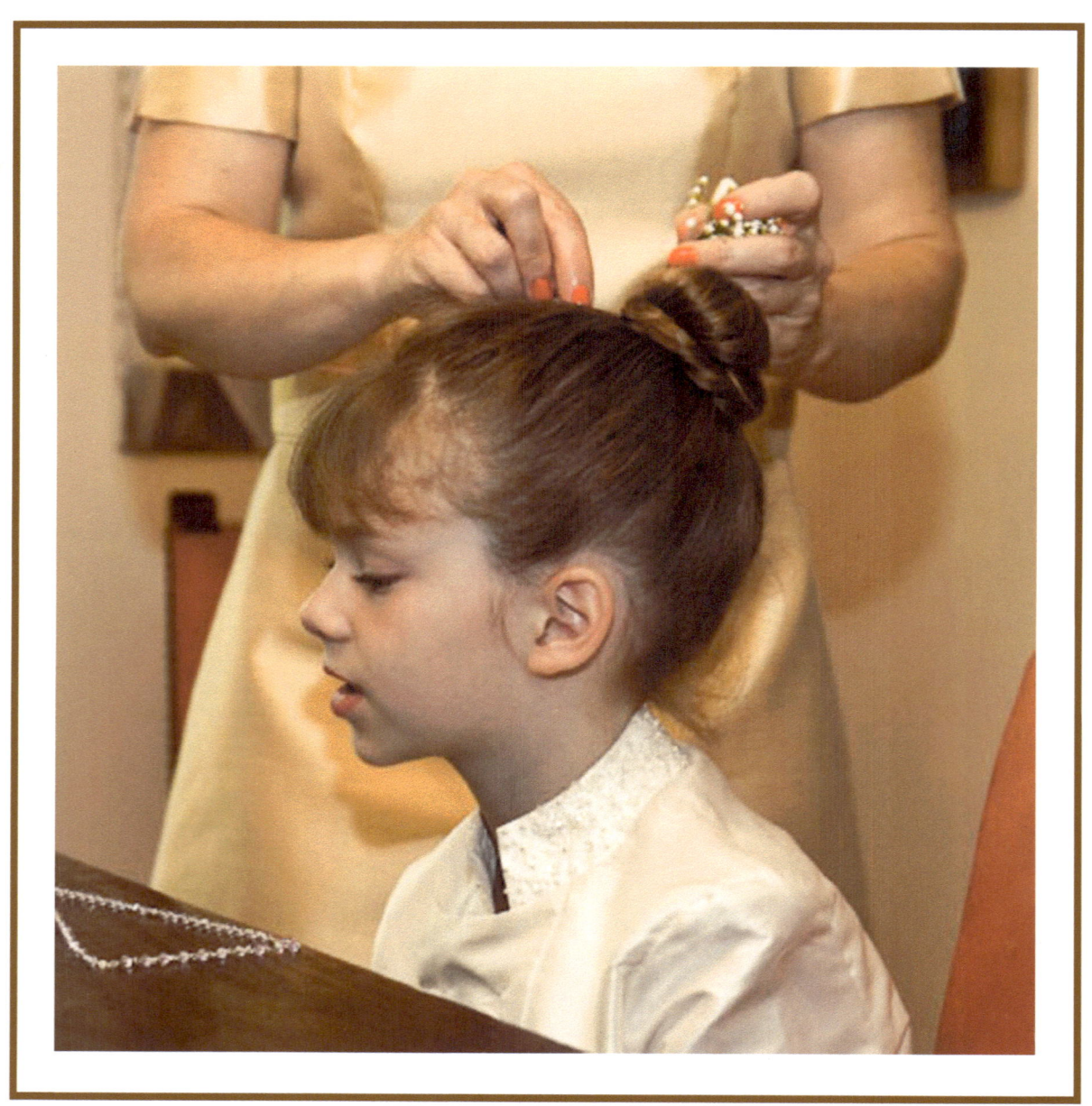

When selecting the head covering, the hairstyle is also important. Simple hairstyles work best on children. Look for styles that feel youthful and sweet. Sophisticated updos are elegant, but most children are not used to the hair spray and gels required to keep the hair in place, and an itchy hairstyle will lead to an unhappy child.

A style that keeps the hair away from the face, so the child doesn't play with it during Mass, is best. For short hair, a few decorative barrettes may be all that's needed. Medium length hair can be pulled back and secured at the crown. Long hair looks elegant and sweet pulled into a ballerina bun. Try out the hairstyle in advance, along with the head covering, if possible, to ensure that everything feels comfortable and stays secure. Consider asking the florist for a wire frame with a few sample flowers to simulate the wreath.

Dress shoes are another important wardrobe accessory for the ceremony. Formal shoes are generally available in leather, patent leather or fabric. It's best to shop for special occasion shoes three to four months before the event, since many popular sizes quickly sell out. Have your daughter practice walking in the shoes so that the soles are less slippery and she feels comfortable in them.

Ballet flats and mary janes are classic dress shoes that always look charming. Some girls may want to wear a shoe with a heel, so if that's the case, look for a slight heel that is easy to walk in and doesn't make a lot of noise. While making Communion is an important step in a child's religious development, it's not an initiation into adulthood. Girls are still young children and not accustomed to walking in high heeled shoes.

There are several other accessories that help complete the Communion outfit. Clothing accessories that help provide the finishing touch include jackets, petticoats, purses, gloves, and socks or tights. Religious accessories such as rosary beads, prayer books and cross necklaces are very personal and may be given as a gift by the godparents.

Many of these accessories are wonderful keepsakes and help turn photographs and other reminders of the day into cherished mementos. However, some parishes discourage accessories because they do not want the children playing with them during Mass. If your church has such a restriction in place, consider bringing the items and taking pictures with the accessories after the ceremony.

Preserving a Communion outfit is a wonderful way to create a family tradition. A simple yet effective way for heirlooming the garment is to store the outfit in a chemical-free cotton garment bag, which should then be stored in a dry dark closet or in a cedar chest. This method of preservation allows the dress to be taken out and looked at from time to time. All items should be cleaned prior to being placed in the cotton bag. Cedar blocks can be used to help ward off moths and other insects. The outfit should not be stored in a plastic bag since the petroleum-based chemicals in the plastic will cause the garment to discolor and deteriorate over time.

Communion is an important rite of passage for a Roman Catholic child. We hope that you and your child will remember this special event, for years to come.

Successfully photographing children during special occasions requires a mix of professionalism and playfulness. We would like to thank several talented photographers for capturing so many treasured moments.

www.CarolBarnstead.com
Tom MacGregor
www.istockphoto.com/John Archer/Eldad Carin/SondraP

Tracy Young is President and self-proclaimed "Chief Princess" of A Little Indulgence. The company offers special occasion dresses and accessories to girls via trunk shows, in-person appointments, a website and select boutiques. If you need an appointment or would like to host a First Communion trunk show, contact us through www.alittleindulgence.com.

www.ingramcontent.com/pod-product-compliance
Lightning Source LLC
Chambersburg PA
CBHW060819090426
42738CB00002B/45